Ra [illegible] She has lived in Devon, Staffordshire and Norfolk, and has worked as a waitress, ice-cream lady, telemarketer and civil servant. She has completed a BA and MA in Creative Writing at the University of East Anglia. Her poems have been published in *Envoi, Staple, The Rialto, Thumbscrew, Reactions, Pretext* and *The Egg Box.*

Come What You Wished For

Ramona Herdman

Egg Box Publishing
Norwich

Egg Box Publishing
25 Brian Avenue, Norwich, NR1 2PH

The Egg Box Web Site Address is:
boxofwords.com

First Published in Great Britain by
Egg Box Publishing 2003

ISBN 0-9543920-1-9

Printed and bound in Great Britain by
Biddles, Guildford

Designed by Alexander Gordon Smith

Many thanks to Ross Sutherland for the refrain 'Come down before you fall down', to Alexina Baird, Julia Bell and Ali Smith for their generous support, and to everybody else who helped with the production of the book.

Thanks to my Tom, my family, my girls.

This one's for Ladyboy.

Come What You

Wished For . . .

1

i.

We are almost the perpetual motion machine:
the formula for what goes in and what's produced
is scarcely less than equal, almost *n*.

Now what lit it is gone.
The heat run off into the frost-web stars.
We can admit we are only fond,

cold hand in hand.
I want him most
over the heads of street cats, grand

in their drawn
lack of expectancy. Their jaws
are calm. They're so thin

over the ribs the fur seems taken in.
They wouldn't dream of rescue,
like I do, walking home

with their abandonment a thumb
stuck in my gullet, claws
in all the soft places, guilty skin.

ii.

The bad cat has come for our breakables.
The bad cat loves us as alarm calls love hangovers.
Come the revolution, he'll be rutting in our carcasses –
ribcages for bondage, tresses for ripping.
The bad cat comes toeing, tip, slipping.
The bad cat comes smiling under the big toe fold
of his chin. He knows us. We are young
and fed and liberal. We let the bad cat in
every time. He takes the bowls of our wineglasses
for boxing gloves. We love him like we love
the storms outside. The rain like bullets,
each pellet confirming they can't get us.
We doze and the bad cat lets us. Our wineskin throats
are of little interest to him. We are fledglings,
each thinking he's the only cuckoo.
The bad cat is immaculate. Everything he ruins is done in
in one motion. He sits among us licking
his barbed penis, unmoved, shining.

2

The angels have come down and written
'Point is who is your best friend?'
They know we'll tell ourselves it was the children.

It's on the pavement, chalk as white as Orion.
No hopscotch, pentagram, game's easy end –
the angels have come down and written.

Walking, after that, fits itself to the rhythm of the question,
on your way to a job you can't mend.
They know we tell ourselves it's for the children.

The angels snicker. They're bastards, all of them.
Sterile, unflinching, unblinded they rend
the truth into what they've come down and written.

If we could swallow it, we would have bitten
off something the size of a star. A grain like one sperm
we tell ourselves will be the children

grows till your belly's the sun. A little
question can split you – what did you want?
The angels have come down and written.
They know we tell ourselves it was the children.

3

I was given a rabbit's foot,
light and hard as chewed paper,
the claws in it moving like the
sharps and flats on a piano,
prickling my thumb.

I was told it was for luck.
This dry, winded, ended thing
like an owl-pellet.
I wondered if something in it was a magnet
that would bring the good
to its opposite pole.

It made me think it must have been
an infant rabbit, to have stood
on so little a foot, the thing
lessened like a hayloft apple,
a shrunken head.
It was impossible not to touch,
to make it run the race of my palm.

I thought it might do the opposite –
ward off harm with its dry grass
dirt smell, its evil lapsed fur.
It was a powerful captured thing.
I thought the rabbits would catch it back
and seeing, that evening, a hare
do the usual abrupt running,
I knew it was a decoy,
felt the crows in the dark trees.
The foot warm and sweaty as a marble in my pocket.

So it was almost a relief when the cat had it,
caught it like a kill from the bedside cabinet,
swallowed it, blinked over it.
It wasn't my plan, but I didn't save it,
I'm not one of those out in the world with a thumbful of rabbit,
the luck, or not, of knowing.

The cat, later that summer, never came back.
Tess said the cars could have had it,
or the foxes.

4

We said 'Let's play' as though
we could decide to pretend.

Then morning's grey through too-thin
curtains. It's four or five AM.
We don't remember what we were dancing about.
We don't know what's been said.
We smile the obvious. I just wish
the synapses flinching in my head
would straighten out, damp down.
We're gentle, as though something hurt. Cloud-slow.
If we could wash our faces into what we feel
they'd fizz like dead TV, unreel like falling snow.

5

Some of us are yet too scared
to take your pills like petals, wet
like the tip of a tongue on the tip
of the tongue.

We watch as you dance blind
tied to the falling trapeze
your hands only capable of holding
the cogs of your own knees.

We have warmed our palms
on the sweat and the open-eyed love
that you let fall like snowy fingertaps
from your foetal highs.

You know you'll fall down,
inevitable as the explosive letdown
of the tingle of the coming
of a sneeze.

You know you'll fall down
when you look down
when it wears off
when you start to care.

You know later
you'll need more touching
than stars hiccuping
in your hair.

Come down please.
We are earthbound.
We are manacled by our knees,
by our belief

in broken bones.
Come down to us,
to limits, bedtimes,
the small things of home.

Come down before you fall down
because if you fall down
we'll never dare
step above our footstools,

root chair on chair
and rocket up, our footprints
corn circles, pebble-dabs on pools.
Whilst you are up,

whilst you are up
the comet-tail of your comedown,
sharp as a lift-shaft,
wavers under you.

Whilst you are up
our palms
shiver like the ultra-violet
cups of caverned mushrooms,

white as the filament
in the unlit throats of doves,
they grab our arms up.
We wave ourselves like handkerchiefs

wanting you to drop.
When you're down we're both morose.
Fetid sweat of fear or hope
smells the same: dead mouse, too close.

O, when you're up
you're very very good.
You are white as a ringlet,
adorable, soft

as the incurl of a shell.
When you are elevated, manic,
sanctified,
I want to make you well.

Come down before you fall down.
Down the fall, so it's shot
like a clay pigeon
and I can see

its lack of threat –
crumble it like powder in my palm
and you can get
more pills.

The moment you're going up for,
that I'm staying down, coming
up with, is the instant
at the salt rim,

the lifted step, the shared bubble
of breath before the first kiss.
The moment when nothing is: the emptiness
that cannot fall.

Come down so you can be going up
slow as a feather, rooted in the
future imperfect, the middle syllable.
The perfect moment before it all.

6

When I'm asked clubbing, all I can think of
is cow-pats of puke on the stairs and that girl,
fifteen, who'd made her own fluffy bikini
and was wearing cat's-eye contacts
that made the skin and the eyeball edges
pale as mouth ulcers.

Headrushes have started to scare me.
As they whip out from under my feet I don't believe,
anymore, that they'll leave the crockery standing,
the bud vase and its bright-eyed daisy.

I used to love it. The ability to plummet.
I'm scared this distaste is the oncreep of age.
Will I be watching my steps forever,
safe?

7

'There are worse things I could do . . .'
Rizzo, *Grease*

It is too late, too late. Yes, go on, laugh.
My foolish armour is wearing silky off –
something like the pink underscrape
of under fish-scales is bleeding through my nape,
that crux and kiss-spot where
my mother lifted me. I grow my hair
with the accumulated wisdom of a trunk of magazines.
There is something wearing off me. Watch the seams
at my elbows and my knees stretch their insides out.
There are these lapses that I'm learning about.
I am too old to hurt myself and heal
in one smooth tumble now – the roll and kneel
and recovery come separate.
Oh bless my over-watchful, twittered heart
that knows itself the beak, birdbrain and breast,
cold-blooded claws and dragon eggs and deadwood nest.
It is too late to play a lightfoot catch,
to launch myself as shuttlecock, to set the match
and let the game blaze up and walk barefoot.
I see the safety-margins round the good.

I see the brink as well as ever, lack the throttle
to war-cry frou-froued over it, full bottle
in my hand, full-gulleted, full well aware.
There was a time I dressed in gold and blued my hair.

I know better now. As the down of ignorance rubs thin
I learn tact like the plus perfect, dress for flattering.
I am altogether more an accomplished human being
and less a scraggy drunken dervish, weeping.

I couldn't want to go the way of thin addled women –
addicted, visionary, still ricocheting.
My wings are burnt. I've learnt to modulate the flying.
I envy the slow learners their pained testing and trying.

8

I have no personal experience of snakes.
I have touched captives,
heavy as emperors, proud as a specific sort of sin.
They are their skins in a way furred things are not.

And a small chevroned one once
woke under my feet as I ran through the grass
to the chicken hut and made my heart
take off like a bumblebee,
stunned me breathless as though I'd hit my jaw
with my own knee, as it tipped itself
like oil off the path.

Thanks be to the snake for that gasp,
that split-second dragon (in the same way
a sneeze is an eighth of an orgasm)
that's kept me in my head, fleet,
lovely bare-legged, seventeen, against a sky-blue
nineteen-fifties sky, all personal experience,
perfect, unbitten.

9

Nights I'm the only one here I get dim and lonesome,
dull and lowdown. I dye my hair. I change the sheets.
I lie there and think what they're missing.
Perfume behind the soft underfold of ear.
The bombs outside would be further, the blue murder
off in a blue moon if he were here.

If he were here, so what? The bed would be overhot,
undersized. Another pair of eyes does not
do away with the desert. They never adore
the right bits. Sometimes I wish I could gingham and brisk
away all the lip gloss and tits, the years
and the polish, the murmurs and spit.

The horses hitched outside know all the stunts.
It's been an old man's rodeo a while now.
Feathers and rhinestones for no real reason
and the endless happy hour waiting for a blazing telegram.
You can can-can till you almost fly –
it won't get you any closer to your man.

They called it a young man's game, this war
and off they went, as beautiful as Icarus.
And vanished in the sky like aeroplanes, turning on a glint,
like Icarus. That Concorde Minotaur six gun roar,
bigger than a baseball game. And we have their young men
holed up here in confusion, in rage and fever.

Last night I dreamt of ants – there wasn't a tree left
in all the treed canyon for mine to nest
and bristle in. I've never felt
so much a lion and I've woken all tooth and maw.
I'm not waiting any longer. It's not twilight anymore.
I'm off to dance with the bombs – it's what the burning in me's for.

10

Up its own curl, interested only in the suck of its tail.
A snail is a whale to itself, a yawing utter of flesh,
filling up all that's left. Its armchair and TV and rum
and Coke and Bounty Bar are all in its mind, behind
the curve of a further whorl in the self-fulfilling
whirlpool of snail. A snail can get antennae up
occasionally. But what's to pick up?
A snail can haul and fail itself to orgasm –
so what? If a snail awoke enough to unfurl
the cold smoke, the stubbed end of itself
and breathe in, it would have to admit
something other than it
and turn crabbed in a corner, suddenly small.

11

Yeah, fair enough carousing, fair enough
the drugs – I know that 'fun' can't do them justice.
And fair as Hell, the early hours, I know.
They're fine as lovers' hair, they flare like laughs
in conversation, fire against the night.
I don't want to deny you delight.
But I don't want you absconding, don't want
you catching pleasures in flight, roses ripped
while ye may. Define 'joy'. Define 'fright'.
Now divide by the result. Don't flinch.
Don't reach for the panacea of the thrill,
the easy chemical. I like you high.
But I like you sober as well. Don't tell
me you could stop if you wanted to. Why
don't you want to? Ever? What is unwell?

12

Drink till you're ill. The restless thrill is necessary forever.
Look to your loved ones – how could you stand a comfortable life together?
How could you stand the waking? The walking and working and walking back?
How live at ease on that pit-pony's primrose track?
Watch the long days going, blowing like grass seeds and the beginnings not coming back.

There's the point where you make the decision. There's the point where you rue it.
There's where you see sense and the huge great holes the wind blows through it.
There's the point of no return, red and black and fair.
There's being too scared to turn and being too gone to care.
There's gin in the afternoons and salt in the ends of your hair.

There's only one way to go. It's signposted, made easy.
We march in our rational rows. Rebellion makes you queasy.
The state will pay your pension. Your children will make you happy.
Keep yourselves busy – focus on rattles and nappies.
It will be different for them – they will be true and happy.

Or we could be great campaigners. We could live on rags and humility.
But how could we ever be sure, in the speed and the glare and humidity?
And how would we know we were right?
Who doesn't howl in the night?
We'd have to be stupidly clear in our sight

and we'd have to think we weren't guilty. Or we could be drunk
all the time.
We could make it on liking our dirt, on thinking conforming's a crime.
On being proud to be hurt.
On parading our keening and blurt.
We could sing, we could lose our shirts.

You know it's not really a choice. You know what you think of all this.
You've already a life and a voice. You've already a therefore and thus.
You know who's them and who's us. You know who's us and
who's them.
We don't take a path on a whim,
we suit how we put in our time.

You live the most suitable life. Who you are leads your feet on the way.
I despise it, but know what I am. I take the ant's clockwork day.
The grasshoppers sing in the night. They air a most beautiful lust
or tell of a willing to fight for a metre of grass-stems and dust.
You know your limits, I trust.

You know your side of the tracks. The trains slice the line in the dark.
The wheels scream a sculpture of sparks. We troop, two by two, to the ark.
We live out our ancestors' lives, but with toasters and radar and pop.
The grass seeds blow off the stems, the walking doesn't stop.
It's easiest two by two. It's lonely, it's a fair cop.

13

I woke up mopped-up, tucked-up, nauseous,
dry inside with aftermath, salted skin.
I'd vaguely been outdrinking all of us.

Most of the night whited-out, glorious –
the lambent blue bag for vomiting in.
I woke up mopped-up, tucked-up, nauseous.

I lost at drinks; rode home victorious,
laurelled with steadying hands, found a bin.
I'd vaguely been outdrinking all of us.

The rain paddled in me, seafront, porous,
puddled in our vodka mug, hand-warm, thin.
I woke up mopped-up, tucked-up, nauseous.

Made pacts, forgave a year's injurious
spat fights. Held hands, palms warm out of the wind.
I'd vaguely been outdrinking all of us.

The morning's sanded, conscious, serious.
I walk home a galleon, swabbed in gin.
I woke up mopped-up, tucked-up, nauseous.
I'd vaguely been outdrinking all of us.

14

I could be an alcoholic, easy.
I could do gin-lovely twilights,
lilac, shading into fuzz like fainting.
I could paint myself disdainful,
powdery as pearl-light, casting
the least painful radiance possible
on the slackening ropes of my neck.
I could drink myself dark as a skinful,
so sodden I half float, the curves above
the surface unlined as a bottle,
the hull of a boat, heeling,
the light feeling its way like the white
of a blind man's stick.
I could drink like those rains
that rain genteel, unchanged for years,
smaller than tears, more like the fizz
of the first of the soda, wetting the
back of your hand like velvet.
I could be an alcoholic.
I could drift, I could sift
downriver like the moonlight rough as
icing-sugar on the ripples. I could sit
in the kiss of sleep like a carious tooth.
The truth drawing me airward every morning,
dredged to the surface, cresting the foaming
hem of the water, hacking, pausing.
The bobbing back up jarring, the last jolting picture show
that I can't help gasping for –
the yo-yo of drowning. Waking spitting, vomiting,
saline and submerged and drummed with thirst.
I could have been an alcoholic
if Daddy hadn't got there first.

15

James' hand on my back, under my top, blind as a drink.
He tells me his secret. He doesn't think
that the office has spread it like spilt tasty ink
and our bored blotter minds, before you can blink,
have licked it up clean as the cat with the cream.
So I tell him, in friendship, I've been told his dream
and he doesn't remember, and he doesn't quite hear
but, several days later, the scratches of fear
have filtered their way to the plate of his head
and he emails me, carefully, asks what he said.

I'll never tell, though I think he's past saving –
too often the floorshow, all of us clapping.
He can carry himself off as the office drunk
condemning us all for our alcopop funk
from the pit where he's lost. Digging and laughing and thirty-six –
too many nights down for it to be easy as sick.
He has a fine disregard for us small broken things watching –
our alarms at home set to be the only alarms of our mornings.
And I'm glad I pressed flesh
with a man prepared to clown his distress.

A man well aware of the black thing following –
calling it pet names, calling it 'darling'.

He's a trouble I left. We all watch him drowning,
watch the rude signs he's waving

and don't want to break anymore
and thank order for our front doors
and warm arms in the bed that is ours
and the smallness of the window
on the terrible, aspiring, dagger-eyed stars.

16

My first of wishes would be to once
be big enough to lean upon.
As though I were a
bluff, a tor, that time
had chawed as dense as was once
a mother's arm, a
limestone-linened bed, upon
which fairytales kept time
below your head, a
dolphin's buoy, the gray neck upon
which princesses are rescued home, time
everlasting, and not just the once.

My second would be to defeat
the coils in your head, doing you in.
I'd give you a wand, a fair
spit at the shits, combat
the years keeping you in tears. I'd dare a fair
comment. I'd have something to say to defeat.
I'd mention the stitched-up in combat.
I'd be worth the trust, in
a fair world, on a fair
ground. I'd arm you for combat
with more than this sparkler, fizzed over your feet.

My third would be to happily
loose you like laughter, ever
away – a balloon after
its hiccup loss, the end
of its string teasing the treetops. After
all, after everything, to love ought to end
pretending, maybe. I want you happy
even without me. Don't want you ever
sucking my toes in tears again; after
something out of me, as if Happy
were a ring I wasn't handing over.
I want you upright in the end.

17

Mr Palfreyman is happiest with birds.
I quite understand, although I do not know his Latin.
In a corner, at a function, something beats distressfully
right up the song of his ribs and pecks at his eyes from their
runny insides.

And I feel it. Standing with him, I protest
I'm no feline, gesture with glass and programme at my broken teeth.
Palfreyman's breath is trained to death, stone-eyed as an elephant
in spats.
We converse. I say, 'How interesting!' and flap for something further
to ask about birds.

He knows he is patronised and penned. The invited expert pinned
and wriggling. Pinioned. He's done enough of this to let me on, to
pay out rope,
to watch me hop and waddle through the amiable hour or so
and not attempt, not hold out crumbs, not whistle. No.

With him beside me I am not least-suited here
(like being not the fattest woman at the ball – I breathe, expand).
Though he is right – still and profound as a woodland pond –
something in him rouses me to roar.

He holds his hollow bones out with such pathos and contempt.
Everyone knows what is meant by his tremble, his sips, his
sideways eye.
I want to tell him to go back to his tower and die.

This half and tactful gathering is merely horrid.
What is awful is to want the safely alien,
the birds that fly and jabber and maybe take but always fly.

He makes me want to drink and dance and blurt, to touch and tell,
at least to try
to believe that someone live can move and live
as truly and as cleanly as the idea of a bird.
He has made himself absurd in his choice of purity.

He is an expert in his field, but what a field!
A place beset, a clearing in the fog and all around
the bipedal swindlers, thumbed wastrels,
earthbound complex yelling fools.

I want to tell him none of us are wicked self-contained and limited
as a clay-beaked rook. He cleans his glasses. I walk away.
The man has saved me from folding myself in the lifeless
simple pages of a book.

18

A man I knew, who cared even for spiders
panicked in the corners of his dark brown house,
set a sticky trap under his floorboards –
a bright bonny blue straightforward peeled plastic thing
for the interruption of and torture of a mouse.

His soft bearded unworldly face and his dry chipped thumbs
careful over the instructions.
He told me afterwards.
What did I do over the head of that soft furry-faced mouse,
held by however many feet he'd ambled on
to the sticky trap's glued tongue?
I feel sick. I want to gulp back any kisses, laughs, notes of affection
but they are flown as balloons, long gone.

I shouldn't want to cancel back and hoard
any bright moments, breaths positive I've given.
He held my hand and took me seriously, handed over
reason after reason. I couldn't listen. I feel sick
to think this could be a necessary torture, a harm to the least,
benefit to us. I feel sick to think of the mouse looking up
at our noises above until the point the legs sink
and it is sunk in stick to its nose, tongue-pink.

He'll have to get it out before it rots,
surrounded by the spiders, various sizes, who advanced to eat it
and stuck around it like fired flowers, tied in their own knots.

19

I wake up knowing I wasn't missed.
I'd left the phone by my clock
so it could whistle regulated breaths
to wake me up.

It would have worked like a fire alarm;
lit me up, got me dressed
had it rung in the night
strung my night to his
told me I was missed
that in my absence I exist.

The morning's messageless;
dialtone unperturbed, uncut.
My voicemail 'You have
          no
new messages'
hypnotises itself six times
asking me to hang up.

All that ever happened, out,
the memorable best
was dropped cold unpleasant kisses
like a bishop dropping wafers
or the wet paws on your lips
of a family pet.

20

I've always scoffed before at others' fears
that lateness meant a bike under a car
that silence meant a hospital's white grip.
I always swore by probability
and what it is sustaining to believe.

But speaking jolly words into the phone
and being glad you're talking to someone
although it is not me, a doubt creeps down
the trackline of the wire into my throat
and after hanging up the thing digs out
and hatches in a fear behind my neck
and waves its wings all round my head and eyes.
You don't call back.

I am reminded of that boy who died
by downing four large packets of Pro Plus.
Sharp caffeine stuttered slashed and stopped his heart
as it had said it would, on the internet.
He wrote several notes as it happened.
One said 'It isn't working yet.'
I wonder if he wanted it to stop
all through the idle research on the web.
He died, all dressed and decent, on his bed.
They found him five days later, all his care
for quietness and cleanliness upset
by the process of rot and the spark that could care
long dead. He didn't live alone.

So when I speak to your answerphone now
I think how, if it were me doing that
I would lift off the handset, let it watch
me swim out into the impossible
from the difficult.

21

He would not thank you if you called him Orpheus
or quoted him the old text, as known as pantomime:
'Thou wilt not cheat death.'
He is no god; the butterfly of breath
is a crumpled receipt in the recycling bin.
Do not quote the déjà vu of myth to him.

He who would not be Orpheus, who lies to us,
O pity him? His love lies wired to a drip. She thins.
He tells a different story now: she did not try,
off that bridge, to cast herself to die.
She winces in the ward's brisk din.
No-one holds hands. Hers are plastered in.

Morphine, compatriot of Orpheus,
has been withdrawn. I'd guess she feels done in.
He reads in the evenings by her side.
He will not look; she need not hide.
He is fiercely blind to accidents, near-ruins.
She will not make an Orpheus of him.

22

He died on Friday.
I've seen the photos, grey and convulsed
and thin as origami.
His bones a burst ribcage
femurs and spine spilt and clotted
piled to start a fire.
Jaw fixed like a biting horse.
Splinters, paper rubbed off at the elbows
dry tendon biting wire.

It took till Thursday
for them to blanch him in the mausoleum
for them to bloat him into cherubim,
face a puffball, reposed, strokable.
I wondered, in the plush stillness,
if the spores would cyclone out
at the push of his cheek;
what they had stuffed him with,
my emaciate infant brother,
to make him wisefaced as sixty
in that hiatus week.

He lived, despite prayer and prediction,
spastic, to thirteen.
He never dried his newborn stuck-down feathers,
or lost his fledgling shivering fits,
his saturated scrawn,
every finger a conflicting cripple.
He ticked like a water-clock
every breath a suck of spittle
loud as straw-bubbles,
the broken wing-beat of his lungs.

It took a week to drain him like a pharaoh.
Set his lips prim as a compact
powder his skin irresistible as a sugar mouse.
Maybe they broke his neck.
I don't know how else they wrenched it back
from its lifelong shudder over his shoulder.
He'd watched his back with shunted eyes
waiting for its twisted pucker
to burst out into wings and spines.
Taste the ache of each bone with your finger
wisdom teeth breaking ranks.

It was like the hiatus before crying,
the lacuna after an unwanted kiss,
the week they took to perfect his head and neck.
They drew satin up to his tied-up chin.
They cut and discarded the rest of him,
a muddled carcass too tangled to lay straight.
Doubly incontinent, vomiting, nose-bleeding
he had never been neat.
His casket is perfectly dovetailed,
heavy wood from the old trees on a residential street.

I don't think of him straight.
I think of him in the hiatus of a spasm,
outflung, white,
floating naked as a knotted hollow crab
in a midnight mausoleum vat,
pummelled in the last physiotherapy
the convulsions' retreat.
Salting down into softness the mouth that did not speak.

The family gentle, amputated
normal, in that hiatus week.

23

I bury my cat in wet sand
like a litter tray. She was no Isis.
She's mewled and baffle-blinked
and licked everything virulent,
lit her tail like a taper
on candles and puffed up
abscesses like fungus
at every scratch.
The evening's hound-dog yellow.
What would eat a cancered cat,
light and straight as balsa wood?
But I bury her deep.
The vet curled her, best he could,
like a paper screw. You
never invested the big ideas
you can't quite pin out
in a toy?

Like loving a box.
There might have been a mind
in her. If you look too closely
at things like that they snap
shut as a gift horse,
smart off to fairyland.
Ever let a kitten shit in your hand
and not dropped it? I did.

24

She has scaled the whole outside of her cage.
Her white-gloved hands hauled her barrister-fat
and she stands at the edge for a hamster-age
her moomin nose, her heavy-horse head
and her hairy lip all perturbed.

These frights are of course minute and absurd.

It makes me bite my heart back
like sick from the back of my throat
that something can fear something little as that.
I offer my hand. I lower her out
of what's shrunk her stupid, tiny and furred.

These frights minute, of course, absurd.

It's like the over-friendly scabbed cats
or the ones that flinch and creep and shrink
on the street, in the cold, round the back of the flats
where no-one's the leisure to swallow and think
even once, that it's sad.

These matters of course, frightening? Absurd.

I watched a hare's oval head hit back
with the fast-moving side of a Micra's wheel.
In a car myself, whatever crack
there was was too far away to feel.
But I watched it skid like a shot bird.

Every minute, these frights. Of course, absurd.

25

Do you know the one about breaking hearts
when all that you meant was a bit of a laugh?
The one that flags, half-cock, half-mast?
The one that you lose the last line of?
The one that jolts the heart
like the smart of the start
of a burn as you lift something hot
and there's nowhere to drop
it and it's all your own fault?

26

She speaks in her sleep in the birdsong creak
of an unoiled brass-wheeled hummingbird wound
for an emperor – a snickering, scales down the stairs,
sweet-pitched sound.

This small-timer found and swaddled and fed
for noises like this, that nest in my head
and sleep in my hand.
Clear as a ring in the plush of my heart.

To have and to hold
and to lie separate
and strain for her breath.

Yet if she left it, folded small by the cumulus sea.
If she swam small, wet-haired as a lemming,
off to the line of dark grey where the sky holds the sea
it wouldn't kill me.

She lies in her sleep or smiles or screams
tongue twisted tight round her sweet sweet dreams.

27

I send you this postcard of Humphrey Bogart
in the ice-cream sandwich fantasy
of many of you, between Lauren Bacall and Marilyn Monroe.

And do I have to say what I have done?

Marilyn laughing, looking sculpted from glossy white chocolate,
a little melted, a little touched,
and Bogart looking down

the fair valley of her neckline,
the primrose, gold-downed road down
to the warmth of the damned.

And Lauren, looking too thin, leaning in,
her catsmile showing her teeth.
You can't photograph her reined-in breath.

Her husband's neck
has the texture of a curdled egg.
An old man who gets what he wants.

What have I done?

This is funny,
you see. This is the old devil,
the old rogue, the life

in the little dog yet.
We all sit up and beg.
We want what's suddenly allowed.

What have I done, oh
what have I done, oh
what have I done now?

They could have cropped out Lauren.
It could have been an icon of simple lech –
but it's a turning away, a something left

like a taste on the back of the tongue.
What's left is what's kept
in mind, not what's done.

Don't make me say it.
Let me come home.

28

She doesn't like her kittens.
She doesn't like the pull
the release through the teats
the way you're supposed to feel.

It's as if her feet have fallen off
and have to be watched forever.
As if a bit could get run over by itself –
the memory of a stoned riverbank summer

or how to whistle – lost.
She's made something now,
something like a sieve to sail.
Her guts around her feet making a row

with their small impossible mouths.
They're the birds come back to haunt her.
She doesn't like their wet-feather tails
and how they have to want her.

29

The bad cat has eaten everyone at number eighteen.
He sits between the nets in the front window like porcelain.
His terrible brown teeth. His terrible sweet breath
so close it makes a pansy on the glass.
His catkin claws hang off every tree.
This is a warning. He could be the last cat.
He could have stolen my teenage dream –
Apocalypse and all the cinemas still running,
bumping my way to Devon in a car not really stolen
since the world would be mine.

The bad cat is as clear in his agenda as the ants.
He knows what he wants,
sitting settled and heavy as a big-screen TV,
as a huge soft tea-cosy over a cauldron,
boiling and spitting, daring you to touch.
He has always known what he does.

I'm waiting for him to spread from number eighteen,
to sit like a fluffed pillow or plague-cross
in every window. This first is an act to follow.
I expect some sort of crude salute
as I walk past his watch-station.
But he moves his head, owl-quiet,
his feet settled, saving himself for the push.
He recognizes no-one to salute or mock –
I could as reasonably expect him to blush.

30

Warm days again. I leave the back door open,
not exactly for the bad cat to come in,
not exactly not. No-one asks.
I think they like the moving light
that the door's glass casts along the inside wall.
It swings like a horror-film mirror
and if it never brings the Candyman in
with the season's first bees maybe that's because
it is the not-reflection of a Dracula.
The door speaks in creaks like ouija.
I could hook it back, but the catch is outside
and if the fog came pussyfooting in
on its powder-puff grey paws
I couldn't risk its touch to get outside
to close the doors.

31

> 'she and me never got any closer together than
> two people just get in bed, which is not much
> closer than two cats on a fence humping . . .'
> Tennessee Williams, *Cat on a Hot Tin Roof*

The bad cat chews cigars, he rolls his Rs,
he purrs, he farts, he roars, he rolls.
He's not a master of his arts. He's not got taste.
He's not got class. He's not a tease. He claws.
He takes. He has no thought for trues and fakes.
He breeds. He keeps the litters up.
No reason to. He eats the pups of other alpha males.
He eats. He bites. He kills. He farts.
He's animal as anyone.
The bad cat loves like a gun, like a submarine.
Like bleach loves germs. Like Mom loves clean.
He loves results. He's not employing you to sit and yap.
It's easier, the up and up, than easing down –
claws work one way. His Lotus hates the lower gears.
He spits cigars. The years and years – what use
in thinking of them? He's still fit
to land on a dime and skewer it like a mouse's eye,
on his own throat-slitting hard four feet.

32

The bad cat is not worried by encroaching stalking age.
He is not saved. Nor loved. Nor laved. Nor sage.
He has not saved a long retirement up
of laps and fires and young punier cats
to lick his paws. His huge split, fossil-grey
historical claws are for now.

He stalks, a naked emperor no-one dares see through.
He knows what it is necessary to know:
the sweet gag of blood, the act of fatherhood,
the cull, the kill, the triumph of and trusting to the will.
He has the gravestone-great flat eyes of an owl.
When he outstares the stars and opens his teeth to howl
it is at the urging of loins and gut. He uses his heart
just to pump the mighty blood.

He'd scorn to be grasshopper or ant.
He'd scorn to moon over want
and possibility and moral circumstance.
The bad cat is led in the dance of the leader
by the lion gene. No forked paths for him.
No labyrinth. His empty eyes look straight.
His shoulders roll, grey breakers pushed
by the tide and the moon.
His time will end. He will not need be mourned.

33

The blind man enters politics –
is good at it. Feels everything an inch off.
Keeps it where it is –
conducts a static sonata
with his glossy, tapered stick.

He keeps order and discipline
close to his chest.
It's put to him that anarchy
is the realm of the angels
where they don't need rules to toe,

where somehow collisions shift
and the chaos of the waves
is a case without knives.
The blind man taps his white finger,
points out we inhabit *lives*,

have an eye to keep on, a tongue, a grip.
He is doing, not hoping, the best
and as for the waves, look at Canute.
He draws unerring routes with his stick in the sand,
plans dams. There are souls,

there's the damned, the wrongdoers
and something to be saved.
'I am personally committed. You will not threaten discipline.'
He's drawn his line. He stands his ground.
He guards the line. There's nothing else.

34

woodlouse, curled like a chocolate shaving
grey as the plastic kit-frames bits twisted from
articulated, downcast, walking humped
like it wants to cut the ground from under it
in a perfect bite of self-defeat
snappable, demure, as tempting to whip the armour from
as any supplicant, knelt contemptible

it's a test
to want to idly unhinge its little ugliness
brings on, on creeping feet
small disappointment, disgust

35

She was clearing out the attic years later –
so sensible, womanly, her fingers broader –
and opening the boxes that her mother
had ordered her pack with the older
dolls as her room filled with plastic needing succour
she found what she had done. The
first box bobbed with heads on wonder-
waves of fairy blonde. The
second was all zombie torsos, fingers
down each other's neckholes – an up yours
her mum never unpacked.

And she told me and laughed and I said
I wouldn't steal the image. And I have.

Also Available from Egg Box Publishing:

'Slips down with all the ease of an innocent-looking white pill.'

Concrete Newspaper

'You get the same whack off these poems as you do when reading Juvenal or Simon Armitage . . . Buy this.'

Martin Newell, of the *Independent*

'A handsome book . . . Richard Evans is talented, intelligent and sensitive.'

George Szirtes